Do You Know? Bodies

NEIL KELLY

Scholastic Children's Books,
Euston House, 24 Eversholt Street,
London NW1 1DB, UK

A division of Scholastic Ltd
London ~ New York ~ Toronto ~ Sydney ~ Auckland
Mexico City ~ New Delhi ~ Hong Kong

Published in the UK by Scholastic Ltd, 2011

Text © Neil Kelly, 2011
Illustrations © Tom Connell, 2011

All rights reserved

ISBN 978 1407 12177 2

Printed and bound in the UK by CPI Bookmarque, Croydon, Surrey

2 4 6 8 10 9 7 5 3 1

The right of Neil Kelly and Tom Connell to be identified as the author and
illustrator of this work respectively has been asserted by them in accordance with
the Copyright, Designs and Patents Act, 1988.

This book is sold subject to the condition that it shall not, by way of trade or
otherwise be lent, resold, hired out, or otherwise circulated without the publisher's
prior consent in any form or binding other than that in which it is published and
without a similar condition, including this condition, being imposed upon the
subsequent purchaser.

Papers used by Scholastic Children's Books are made from woods grown in
sustainable forests.

DO YOU KNOW...

- who was the tallest man ever?

- what your brain is made of?

- which body system is nine metres long?

No? Well keep reading and you'll soon find out...

Your Brilliant Body

Your body is amazing. It is a living, breathing, moving marvel! As well as keeping you alive, it also provides you with your five senses: sight, hearing, touch, taste and smell.

Your body is made up of lots of different parts...

• **Your muscles help you to move around.**
• **Your skin keeps your body warm and dry and holds it together.**
• **Your skeleton acts like a frame for your body to hang from as well as being a case to protect it.**
• **Your organs, such as your heart and lungs, work hard day and night to keep you alive.**

All of these parts, and many more, work together to make an incredible, natural machine.

The Body

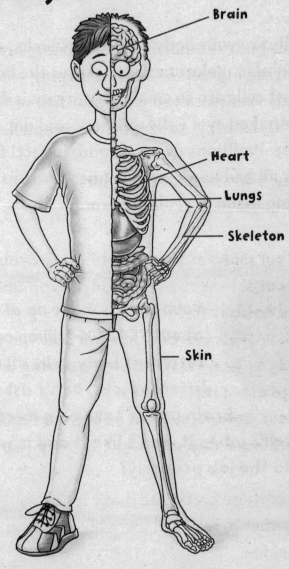

Brain

Heart

Lungs

Skeleton

Skin

Spectacular Cells

Cells are your body's building blocks, and they also make energy to power the body. Most cells are so small they are invisible to the naked eye! Cells wear out and die all the time – millions every second, in fact! But it's not all bad news, as new ones are constantly being made to replace them.

Your body is made up of about 75 to 100 trillion cells! Different body cells all do different jobs. Don't ask a brain cell to take on a liver cell's job — it won't like it and it won't do the job properly!

The **TINIEST CELL** in your body is a brain cell that helps you to detect different types of smells. They are very, very small — you could fit 100 of them on a pinhead!

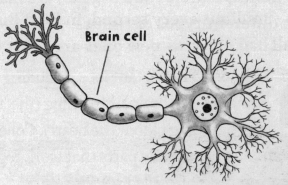

Brain cell

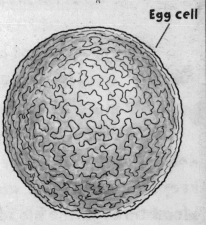

Egg cell

The **BIGGEST CELL** in the body is a woman's egg cell. It's still very small though — about the size of a grain of rice.

Super Systems

Cells group themselves together into stretchy, sheet-like tissues – not the kind you blow your nose on! Your body parts, such as your bones, muscles and organs, are made from different types of tissues.

Organs do important jobs, including thinking (the brain), breathing (the lungs) and pumping blood (the heart). Collections of organs and other body parts that work together to carry out tasks are called systems.

For example, your bony skeleton is a system that works with your muscles to support and move your body. Your digestive system breaks down your food, your respiratory system keeps you breathing, and your heart pumps blood through the blood vessels of the circulatory system.

Meanwhile, your busy nervous system zaps messages backwards and forwards between your brain and your body, including sights, sounds, smells and sensations such as heat, cold and pain (ouch!).

When you have a cold, the immune system releases an army of germ-killing cells to fight off the infection — hooray!

Your Skeleton

Let's begin looking at how your body works by uncovering the under-the-skin secrets of your bone-tastic skeleton...

Reasons Why Your Skeleton is Bone-tastic!

4. It's made up of lots of bones – more than 200, in fact. Some bones are large, some are small and some are really, really tiny, but they are all important and do different jobs.

3. Your skeleton gives your body its shape. Without it, you'd just be a shapeless, blobby bag of organs!

2. It lets you move around. Your muscles are attached to your bones – the muscles pull on the bones, making them move.

1. Your skeleton protects your soft, squishy internal organs, such as the brain, lungs and heart.

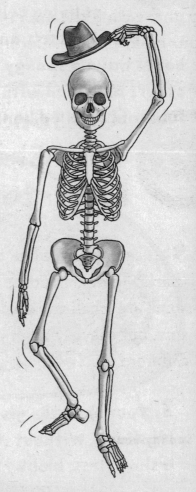

Do You Know?

Bones are not solid all the way through like tree branches! They are made of living cells and contain blood vessels and nerves. Some bones have a spongy centre while others are filled with a jelly-like substance called bone marrow.

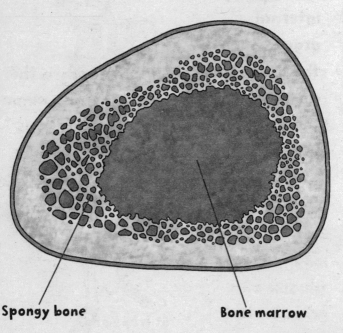

Spongy bone

Bone marrow

The **BIGGEST BONE** in your body is in your leg. It is called the femur, or thighbone. On average, the length of each person's femur is about a quarter of their height.

Femur

The **SMALLEST BONE** in your body is the stirrup bone in your ear. It gets its name because it looks like one of the stirrups that you put your feet in when riding a horse — only it's much smaller! It is just 0.25 cm long — about the size of a grain of rice!

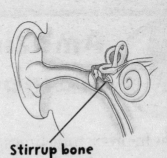

Stirrup bone

Bony Brainbox

You may think that your skull is one big, solid bony brain-protector, but you'd be a headcase to believe that! A human skull is actually made up of 22 bones that are joined together. The top part, called the cranium, is formed from eight large, flattish bones. The face is made up of 14 bones. Useful holes in the skull let air into the lungs and sound into your ears. Your eye sockets are spaced just far enough apart for your eyes to be able to judge length, width and how far things are away from you!

Amazing Brainbox Facts

2. In prehistoric times, getting ill could be a real headache! People believed they could cure you by making a hole in the skull to let out the evil spirits they believed were making you ill. Ouch!

1. **Experts can make up the face of a person who lived thousands of years ago by building up layers on clay on the top of the person's skull.**

The Skull

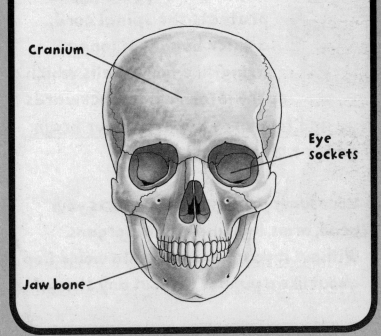

Cranium

Eye sockets

Jaw bone

The Backbone

Your S-shaped backbone, or spine, is made up of 33 small, spiky bones called vertebrae, stacked on top of each other. They allow your backbone to move from side to side, enabling it to twist, bend and turn your upper body.

DO YOU KNOW?

Your super-supple spine protects the spinal cord, a thick bundle of long, string-like nerve cells which carry information backwards and forwards between your brain and the rest of your body.

Your super-strong spine supports your head, arms, legs and internal organs. Without it your head and limbs would flop about like a puppet without any strings!

The Ribcage

Your ribcage is made of 12 pairs of ribs attached to your spine that protect the organs of the upper chest – the heart, lungs, liver and stomach. They have stretchy muscles in between them that contract (shorten) and relax (lengthen again) to help the lungs inflate (fill up with air) and deflate (push out air) during breathing.

On the Move!

Your long, upper-arm bone has a ball-like knob on the end of it that fits into a socket in the shoulder bone. This allows you to swing your arm about in any direction and extend it to lift objects. Your small, delicate hand bones allow you to carry out tricky tasks. Without these tiny bones, you couldn't draw, write, paint, text or play a musical instrument!

Leg bones carry your body's weight, so they have to be bigger and stronger than arm bones. At the top, they join onto the saddle-like pelvis – a group of fused (joined together) bones that include your hipbones. The pelvis carries the push of the legs to the upper body, moving you along. At the bottom, the foot bones take the body's weight and push it off the ground as you walk.

The Skeleton

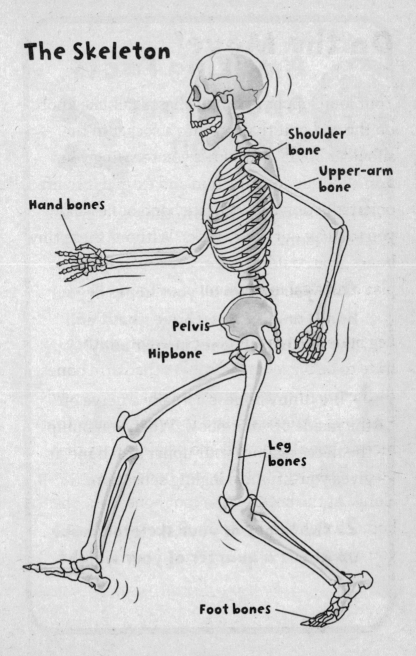

Shoulder bone

Upper-arm bone

Hand bones

Pelvis

Hipbone

Leg bones

Foot bones

Amazing Facts About Your Skeleton

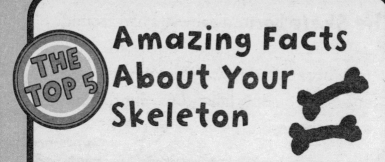

THE TOP 5

5. The strongest bone in the skeleton is the jawbone.

4. If you add up all your bones in your hands and feet, you have about half the number of bones in your body!

3. The funny bone is actually a nerve on the inside of your elbow. When you bump the nerve against your upper arm bone, it gives you a funny tingling sensation.

2. The bones of your skeleton make up about a quarter of your weight.

1. When you were a baby you had around 270 bones. Lots of these bones join together as you grow. By the time you are an adult, you only have 206 – but that's still a lot of bones!

The world's biggest human skeleton belonged to the world's tallest ever man — Robert Wadlow from the USA. He was born in 1918 and died in 1940, aged only 22. He grew to a whopping 2.72 m (8ft 11ins) — about three-quarters of the height of a double-decker bus!

Do You Know?

When Two Bones Meet...

... a joint is formed. Joints give your skeleton flexibility, so that you can stretch, twist and bend. If you didn't have joints, you'd have a very stiff life – you wouldn't be able to touch your toes, turn your head, kick a ball or even hold a knife and fork!

Joint Facts

4. Joints work in different ways. Some joints, like the ones in your elbows and knees are like door hinges, while others, like the joints in your wrists and ankles, glide over each other like rollers. Ball-and-socket joints, like the ones in your shoulders and hips, allow your arms and legs to move in circles.

Knee Joint

3. Bones are held together at either side of a joint by ligaments, which are like very strong rubber bands.

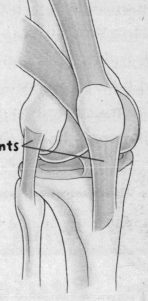

Ligaments

2. People who have very long, stretchy ligaments can do amazing things like put their feet behind their ears – luckily for them, ears are used for hearing and not smelling!

1. Saying someone is 'double-jointed' means a person has very stretchy ligaments — they don't actually have extra joints.

Muscle Power

Bones and joints wouldn't be much use without some muscle power! Muscles are attached to your bones and joints. They contract (shorten) and relax (lengthen) to move your body around. Muscles are made up of bundles of thin strands, a bit like rubber bands, that are packed tightly together. If you've ever eaten a nice juicy steak, this is what muscle looks like. Steak is made from the muscle tissue of a cow.

THE TOP 3

Reasons Why Muscles Are Marvellous

3. Muscles make it possible for us to walk, run, jump and do every other activity you can think of!

2. Some muscles do jobs automatically — you don't even have to think about it! Super-strong heart muscles pump blood around your body, without you knowing it.

1. You couldn't laugh, speak or frown without the muscles in your face! When a face muscle contracts, it pulls the skin of your face and so changes your expression.

THE TOP 4

Must-Know Muscle Facts

4. Your jaw muscle can press your jaws together with a force that's equal to the weight of a fully grown man. That's some serious chomping power!

3. Grinning uses around 17 face muscles, but being grumpy is harder work — a frown uses about 43 muscles!

2. Your eye muscles are your busiest muscles – they move more than 100,000 times a day!

1. Stretchy, rope-like cords called tendons attach your muscles to your bones.

Do You Know?

Here's a timeless tale about a tendon. Your Achilles tendons are in your heels. They are the biggest tendons in your body. They attach your lower-leg muscles to your feet. They are named after the legendary Greek hero, Achilles. Achilles was invincible apart from one weak spot in his heel. His enemies killed him by shooting an arrow into it. Nasty! So whenever we talk about someone's weak spot — like being bad at maths — we call it their Achilles heel!

Life-giving Lungs

Your body is surrounded a mixture of gases called air, and this is a very good thing! Air contains a gas called oxygen. Your cells need oxygen to turn the food you eat into energy. To get oxygen into your body, you use a clever set of body parts called the respiratory system. This includes your nose, mouth, throat, windpipe and your two lungs. Here's how it works...

Breathing In

Air is sucked in through your mouth or nose. It goes down into your windpipe and into your lungs. Your lungs are like two big, folded, spongy bags – surrounded by lots of tubes called blood vessels. Oxygen passes into these blood vessels and travels around your body in your blood.

Breathing Out

When the blood vessels in your lungs take in oxygen, they pass back a gas called carbon dioxide. It's a good swap, as your body needs to get rid of this gas! The carbon dioxide travels back up your windpipe and is breathed out by your nose or mouth.

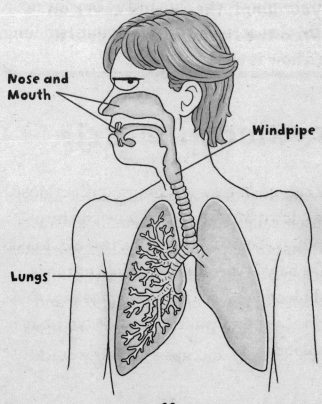

Nose and Mouth

Windpipe

Lungs

Breathtaking Lung Facts

2. You take over 600 million breaths in your lifetime.

1. If you opened up and unfolded your lungs, they would cover an area the size of a tennis court!

The Hiccup Muscle

Underneath your lungs is a big, sheet-like strip of muscle called the diaphragm. It contracts (shortens) to help you breathe in and relaxes (lengthens) again, to let you breathe out. Sometimes it gets a bit out of control and won't stop shortening – this is what causes hiccups! Usually, hiccups stop fairly quickly, but not always – an American waitress named Lucy Macdonald hiccupped non-stop for two years between 1963 and 1965!

Voice Power

As you breathe out, air passes over folds in your throat called vocal cords. The air makes these folds vibrate, or wobble, very fast. This is what produces the sound of your voice, from the quietest whisper to the loudest singing!

You Have to Have a Heart...

...Or you'd die! Your heart is a squeezing, pumping muscle that keeps blood moving round and round your body. The blood travels in the circulatory system which is made up of long, tubes called arteries and veins that spread out to all the parts of your body.

Arteries carry blood that's full of oxygen away from your heart so that the oxygen can be used up by your cells to make energy.

Veins carry the blood back to the lungs to be refuelled with oxygen once your cells have used it up – a bit like filling up a car with petrol!

Hearty Facts

3. Your heart sits between your lungs, slightly to your body's left side.

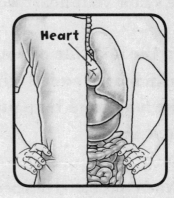

Heart

2. Your heart has two halves, each of which has an upper and lower chamber, like the top and bottom floors of a house.

1. A clever one-way valve acts like a trapdoor between the upper and lower chambers, keeping blood moving and stopping it flowing backwards.

Pumping Power

Here's how your heart works...

1. The left side of your heart fills up with blood loaded with oxygen from the lungs and then pumps it around your body.

2. When this blood has been around your body and has delivered all of its oxygen it enters the right side of your heart.

3. The right side of your heart then pumps this blood, which is now filled with carbon dioxide, back to the lungs.

4. Your lungs remove carbon dioxide from your blood and refuel it with oxygen. The blood then passes back into the left side of your heart to be pumped around the body. Amazing!

The Heart

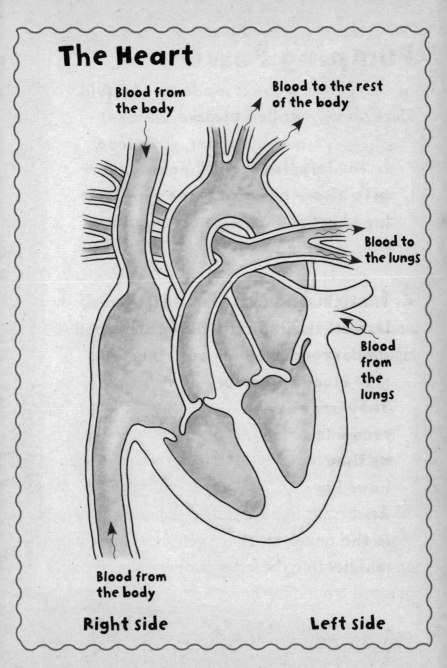

Blood from the body

Blood to the rest of the body

Blood to the lungs

Blood from the lungs

Blood from the body

Right Side

Left side

Do You ? Know

Blood is made up of liquid called plasma, which is mainly water, with food particles sloshing around in it. There are also three types of blood cells floating in this liquid.

1. **RED BLOOD CELLS** are bright-red, button-shaped cells that carry food and oxygen around your body, and give blood its colour.
They are easy to recognize as they have big dent in the middle!

2. WHITE BLOOD CELLS are round and spiky, and larger than the red blood cells. They are your body's main defence against germs.

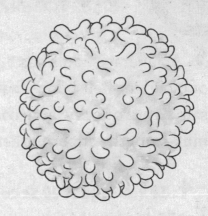

3. PLATELETS are broken-off bits of cells that help the blood to clot (stick together) and form scabs on cuts and wounds.

Blood Facts

5. An average adult has 5 litres (9 pints) of blood in their body. That's about the same as two really large containers of milk from the supermarket!

4. It takes just 20 seconds for a red blood cell to drop off its load of oxygen and return to the heart.

3. Your heart can pump your blood all the way around your body in just one minute.

2. In an average lifetime your heart beats 3,000 million times...

1. ...and pumps over 300 million litres of blood – enough to fill 5,500 large swimming pools!

If you lose a lot of blood, doctors can give you a transfusion — an injection of someone else's blood.

Hundreds of years ago, doctors tried to give people transfusions of animal blood! Patients usually died because the human and animal blood didn't mix. Instead, it clumped together inside their blood vessels, blocking the flow of blood to their cells. Nasty!

The Brilliant Brain

Blood provides your body's systems with food and oxygen to make energy, but it's your brain that tells your systems what to do! There's no doubt about it – the brain is the boss. It may look like a lump of blobby jelly, but it tells your body how to move, and controls your thoughts and feelings. It's also in charge of the things you don't think about, like digesting your food and breathing.

Mind-Boggling Brain Facts

3. The thinking part of your brain – the cerebrum – looks like crinkly, crumpled paper. It's also where your memory lives!

It has two separate but linked halves. The left side of your brain is used for language and maths, the right side is used for artistic things like music and painting.

2. The left half of the brain controls the right side of the body and the right half controls the left side. Nobody knows why — weird!

1. Your brain carries out billions of calculations each day and still finds the time to create dreams when it shuts down for the night!

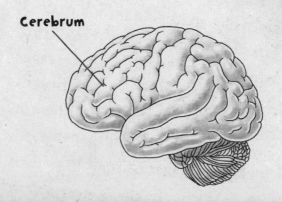

Cerebrum

More Bits of Your Brilliant Brain

THE CEREBELLUM is a ball-shaped blob at the back of the brain. It controls your movements, gets your muscles to work together and helps you to balance. You couldn't run, jump or ride a bike without it!

THE BRAIN STEM looks like the thick root of a plant, but the brain stem has an important job to do. It links your brain to the spinal cord, which carries millions of messages backwards and forwards between your body and your brain. The brain stem organizes all these messages, like a super-fast computer!

The Brain

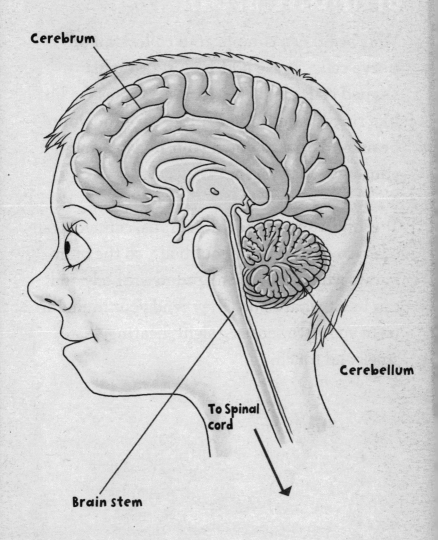

Cerebrum

Cerebellum

To Spinal Cord

Brain stem

Nervous Neurons

Your brain is a complicated collection of nerve cells. These odd-looking, starfish – shaped cells send electrical messages – a bit like tiny flashes of lightning – around your brain and up and down your body through your nervous system.

The long, thin nerves, or neurons, connect your brain to every part of your body, so the brain knows what is going on around the body and can tell it what to do. They send your brain info from your five senses – sight, hearing, taste, smell and touch.

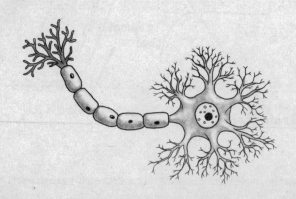

Neurons also send instructions from your brain to your muscles, telling them to move. If you accidently touch a hot kettle with your hand, it's your neurons that tell your brain to move your hand away fast!

Things You Probably Didn't Know About Nerves

2. Electrical messages zoom around your nervous system at about 430 kph (270 mph) – faster than a super-speedy racing car!

1. In total, you have a staggering 100 billion neurons in your body.

Seeing is Believing

Your brain receives information about the world through your five senses. Sight is one of the most important senses.

Your eyes gather patterns of light and send signals through the nervous system to the brain. Your brain then works out what the eyes are seeing.

How Do You See Things?

1. Light enters your eye through a hole at the front called the pupil. It passes through the lens, which acts like the lens in a pair of glasses. This focuses the light patterns and flips them – upside down – onto the back of the eye.

2. At the back of the eye, special cells pick up what you see and change these light patterns into electrical messages.

3. These electrical messages are zapped down the optic nerve at the back of the eye to the brain. The brain flips the patterns the right way up and stores them like pictures in a camera!

Do You Know?

Sometimes the brain sees only what it expects, or wants, to see. So you could be missing something that's actually there, or seeing something that isn't!

Good Vibrations

Your ears are just part of the clever system that enables you to hear sounds. They act like fleshy satellite dishes, catching different sounds and directing them into openings in the side of your head called ear canals.

How Do You Hear Things?

1. Sounds make vibrations in the air.

2. These vibrations travel through the air and into your ear canal and hit your eardrum, making it vibrate as well.

3. Three small ear bones rest on the eardrum and pass the vibrations into curled-up, snail-like tube called the cochlea.

4. Tiny hairs inside the cochlea pick up the vibrations and change them into electrical messages, which are sent to the brain.

5. The brain decodes the signals into the sounds we hear, from the quiet purring of a cat to the loud noise of a car engine.

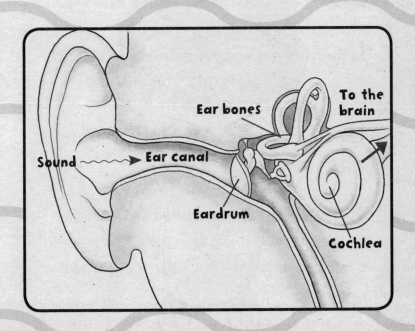

Ear bones

To the brain

Sound

Ear canal

Eardrum

Cochlea

Taste's Terrific!

Without a sense of taste, life would be pretty
dull. Eating would be no fun – ice cream,
chocolate, pizza and curry would all taste
of nothing. Or like cardboard – which is
probably worse!

Your tongue is covered in tiny bumps called taste buds. They can pick up four main tastes – sweetness (chocolate and biscuits), saltiness (salty chips), sourness (too much vinegar on those chips!) and bitterness (yucky Brussels sprouts).

Nerve cells in your taste buds send taste messages to your brains so it can work out what you're eating.

THE TOP 2

Tasty Facts

2. Your tongue doesn't just taste things - it also helps to make the sounds we use in everyday speech. Without, it you couldn't talk properly!

1. Your sense of taste is linked to your sense of smell.

Sensational Smells

From the mouth-watering smell of tasty food to the stink of pongy poo, smells are powerful sensations!

A smell is just a few very, very small pieces (or particles) of something that have found their way up your nose. These particles hit thread-like cells on the inside of your nose, which send the smell messages to the brain.

These cells also help to detect tastes. Particles of food float up your nose, bump into the threads and send taste messages to the brain.

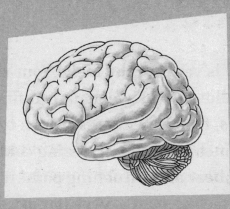

The brain works out what the smell or taste is, comparing it to all of the different records in its memory, from fragrant flowers and freshly baked bread to whiffy fish and stinky old trainers.

One thing's for sure – your sense of smell (and taste) is not something to be sniffed at!

Touchy Feely

Your body is very touchy feely! Your sense of touch allows you to feel many different sensations, from the lightest touch to the hardest pinch, as well as freezing cold, scorching heat and throbbing pain! It might hurt, but feeling pain is very important – it is your body's way of telling you there is a problem, or of stopping you from injuring yourself.

Your body contains special cells that can feel different sensations, such as heat, cold, pain, touch and pressure. Your skin has lots of these cells.

How Do You Feel Things?

1. When a sense cell detects a sensation, it sends a message to your brain.

2. Your brain decodes this message to find out what type of sensation your body is feeling.

3. Your brain works out where in the body the sense message came from.

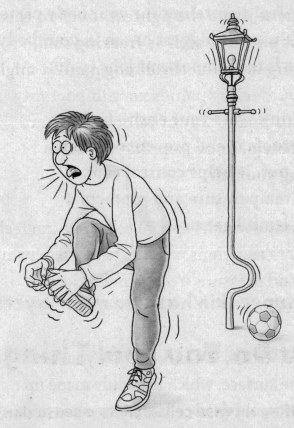

So, if you walk into a lamppost and stub your toe, you'll feel pain in your foot. Ouch!

Why You Have to Love the Skin You Are In

Your skin is more than just a fleshy, stretchy, touchy-feely container for your body parts! Your skin is the biggest organ in your body and has lots of important jobs to do.

Your skin covers your entire body. It waterproofs it and prevents it from drying out. It helps control your body's temperature and protects it from harmful germs.

Your super skin has two main layers.

1. A TOUGH, OUTER LAYER you see on the surface, which is mainly made up of nasty, old dead cells that are shed and replaced by new cells underneath.

2. A LOWER LAYER

which contains blood
vessels, sense cells, sweat
glands (a gland is a small
organ) and hairs. If your
skin gets damaged, it heals
the wounds, forming scabs
that fall off as new skin grows.

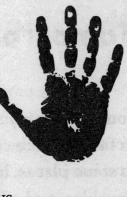

When you are hot, your hair lies flat against the skin to let sweat escape, taking heat with it.

When you are cold, your hairs stand up, like 'goose bumps', to trap warm air next to your skin. Brrrrrilliant!

Hair Today, Nails Tomorrow!

You're probably a lot hairier than you think – in fact, you are covered in the stuff! It's thin in some places, like on your forearms or your knuckles, and a lot thicker in others, such as on your head. Hair isn't just for styling, hair helps to control your body's temperature.

Your hair and nails are made out of the same tough material called keratin.

Without nails, you'd have very sore, squished fingertips. They protect the ends of the fingers and toes and are a bit like an animal's claws. You can use them for scratching your nose, you can paint them if you're feeling artistic, or you can chew on them if you're stressed – not a good idea as they taste horrible!

DO YOU KNOW

• The **LONGEST HAIR** on record belonged to Mata Jagdamba of India. Her hair grew to 423 cm long — about the length of an average-sized car.

• The **LONGEST NAILS** belonged to Sridhar Chihall — another Indian record-breaker. He stopped cutting his fingernails in 1952. By 1995, the nails on his left hand were 574 cm long — the length of a small van!

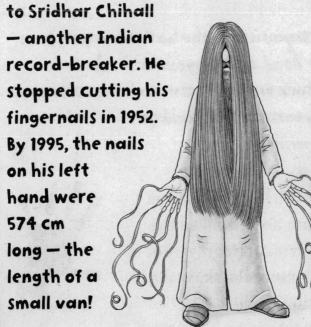

Strange Skin, Hair and Nail Facts

6. If you stretched it out an average adult's skin would cover the area of a single bed.

5. If you are in the bath for a long time, the dead cells on your skin's surface absorb water. This makes the surface of your skin swell and go all wrinkly!

4. The hair you see on your body is called the hair shaft. It grows out of a tube in the skin called a hair follicle.

3. Hair keeps our heads warm — but we cut and style it so we can look cool!

2. Nails grow quite slowly. If left uncut for a whole year, they would be about 2.5 cm long (about as long as your big toe).

1. Nails like the summertime! Fingernails grow faster than toenails, but both grow more quickly in hot weather.

Fantastic Food and Digestion

Food is fantastic – it's tasty, yummy and stops your stomach from grumbling! In fact, your body just can't do without it. It gives you the fuel you need power your systems, as well as providing all the materials your body is made of.

It's your digestive system's job to digest food – to break it down and turn it into fuel and raw materials your body can use. Your digestive system starts inside your mouth.

Munching and Mashing

When you put food into your mouth, your teeth chomp it up into tiny pieces. Your tongue pushes the pieces of food around your mouth, mixing it up with saliva (spit) so you can swallow it more easily.

Do You Know?

Children have 20 "milk" teeth. These fall out and are replaced gradually by a permanent set of 32 teeth, each with its own important job to do.

The Stomach and the Intestine

Once the food's all nicely mashed up, your tongue rolls it into a ball and pushes it to the back of your mouth. The food then passes down a tube in your throat and into your stomach.

Stomach Churning

The stomach is like a large bag surrounded by muscles. The muscles squeeze the stomach to help mush up the food and mix it all together. Acid in the stomach dissolves the food and turns it into a foul-smelling liquid. The stomach is lined with a thick, slimy mucus to protect it from the acid.

Inside the Intestine

After a few hours in the stomach, the squidgy slop is squirted through a hole in the bottom of the stomach into a coiled tube called the small intestine, or gut. The gut is thin but it's also very long – roughly four times the length of your body. It absorbs useful substances from the food into the blood. From here they are sent to a big, triangular organ called the liver...

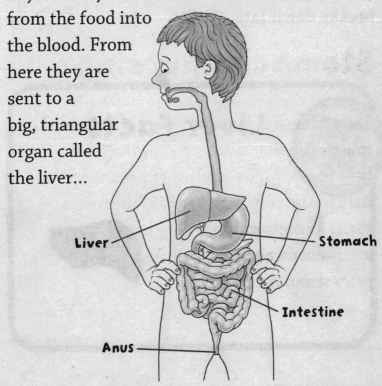

Liver

Stomach

Intestine

Anus

The Sorting Organ

The busy liver is a bit like a post-office sorting machine – it separates out the absorbed substances and sends them off to different parts of the body. It also gets rid of substances the body doesn't need and makes a nasty green substance called bile, which breaks down fats. Yuck!

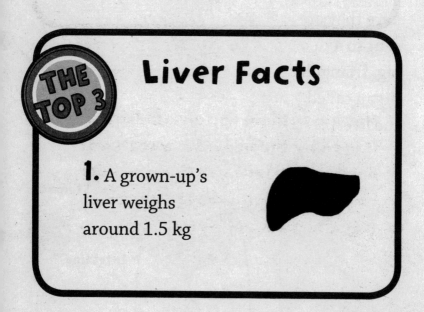

THE TOP 3

Liver Facts

1. A grown-up's liver weighs around 1.5 kg

2. As well as acting like a sorting machine, the liver can also store stuff that your body needs, such as vitamins.

3. Bile may be a bit gross, but it can be recycled. When the bile has broken down all the fats it can, chemicals in the bile are absorbed back into the blood and are made into more bile.

Not everything you eat and drink is used by the body. So, what's left once your small intestine and liver have done their job? It's our old friends... poo and wee!

Waste Products

Poo and wee might be a bit gross, but they are really very interesting. Pooing and weeing is your body's way of getting rid of some of the things it doesn't need.

What is Poo?

Poo is made up all the solid things that your body can't digest, such as hard bits of vegetables, skins from fruit, and seeds. This waste is moved through your gut, called your intestine, by muscles in your tummy. The intestine soaks up the water in the waste, drying it out. Finally, it passes out of your anus – the hole in your bottom – and splashes down in the toilet as brown, pongy poo. Hooray!

THE TOP 3

Things You Probably Didn't Know About Pooing and Farting

3. Farts, or whatever you might call them, are your body's way of getting rid of any air that you might have swallowed. Farts smell because swallowed air mixes with stinky chemicals given off by the bacteria in your gut.

2. Three quarters of your poo is made up of water. Of the rest of it, one third is made up of dead bacteria. Yuck!

1. An average child produces 150 g of poo each day. That's over 50 kg a year!

Making Wee

As your blood travels around your body it passes through a pair of bean-shaped organs – called the kidneys that remove waste and any extra water from the blood. The clean blood passes back into the bloodstream, while the waste and water form a smelly liquid called urine – that's wee to you!

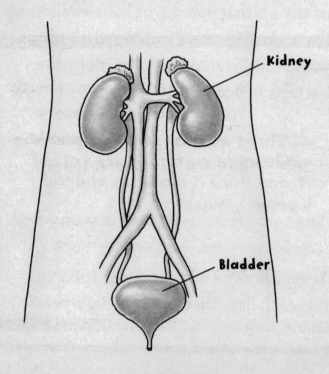

Kidney

Bladder

The wee passes out of the kidneys, down some tubes and into a stretchy bag called the bladder. Muscles hold the wee inside the bladder until you are ready to get rid of it. That's unless you hear a really funny joke and it happens by accident!

A grown-up can wee as much as one to two litres every single day. That's more than 40,000 litres in a lifetime!

Some people believe that drinking wee can be good for your health. Yuck ... don't try it!

Digestion Facts

4. Make sure you drink water several times a day – you lose a lot of it when you wee, sweat and even just by breathing, so you need to replace it. Don't dry up!

3. The digestive system is the longest set of organs in the body — if you unravelled it all, it would measure over 9 metres in length — about the length of a bus!

2. Your guts are full of lots of tiny animals called bacteria. Some bacteria are nasty and

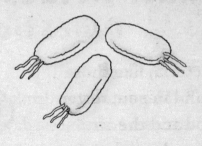

can make you ill, but lots of them are useful and help you digest your food.

1. Your poo is also full of bacteria — this is why it is so whiffy! The bacteria make substances and gases that smell bad and can be harmful.

This is why you should always wash your hands after using the toilet!

Under Attack!

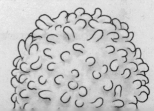

Bacteria, like those
found in poo, rotten
food and the air
around us are tiny
little living creatures,
too small to be seen with
your eyes. If they get into
your body they can make you ill.

Fortunately, you have a heroic army
of spiky soldiers to protect you
– the white blood cells of your
immune system.

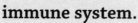

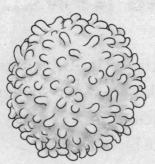

How Does Your Immune System Work?

1. When germs get into your body through cuts and scratches, your white blood cells go into action.

2. These strange, spiky cells rush to the wound and launch themselves into battle.

3. They destroy as many germs as they can by swallowing them up!

The Bad News...

Sometimes the germs defeat the white cells. The yellow stuff you see coming out of an infected cut is pus – a yucky fluid made out of dead white blood cells!

Bodies Quiz

1. How many bones do you have in your skull?

 a) 22
 b) 1
 c) 200

2. What is the name of the gas that your cells need to turn food into energy?

 a) carbon dioxide
 b) helium
 c) oxygen

3. What colour is bile?

 a) red
 b) green
 c) blue

4. Where is wee stored before you get rid of it?

    a) in your bladder
    b) in your brain
    c) in your heart

5. What did American waitress Lucy Macdonald do for nearly 2 years?

    a) cough
    b) hiccup
    c) fart (!)

6. Which part of your body controls your movements?

    a) your heart
    b) your brain
    c) your muscles

7. How many neurons do you have in your body?

    a) 300
    b) 12
    c) 100 billion

8. What do your white blood cells do?

a) fight infection
b) carry oxygen around your body
c) carry food around your body

9. Which type of cells have a big dent in the middle?

a) brain cells
b) prison cells
c) red blood cells

10. What do your veins do?

a) fight infection
b) carry blood around your body
c) carry electrical messages to your brain

INDEX

Also available...

Jam-packed
with facts!

Coming Soon...

Do You Know? Extreme Wheels
Do You Know? Sharks